PRAISE FOR JACQUELINE PIRTLE

"Jacqueline takes you always directly to what you are ready to see or experience."

— LONGTIME CLIENT AND READER

"It is liberating to face your own blocks and to be finally free of the weight that they have caused for many years. And while for me the changes I'm experiencing are noticeable and real, I still feel like myself. Just a more sure self."

— LONGTIME CLIENT AND READER

"Jacqueline makes me BELIEVE I can be and live a joyful and magical existence every new day of my life!"

— LONGTIME CLIENT AND READER

The *365 Days of Happiness* bestselling author

JACQUELINE PIRTLE

THE SILVER LINING

AND HOW TO FIND IT

COPYRIGHT

Copyright © 2021 Jacqueline Pirtle
www.FreakyHealer.com

All rights reserved. No part of this book may be reproduced or transmitted in any form or by any means, electronic or mechanical, including photocopying, recording, or by any information storage and retrieval system without the written permission of the publisher, except where permitted by law.

ISBN-13: 978-1-955059-35-0

Publisher: Freaky Healer

Editor-in-chief: Zoe Pirtle
All-round Support: Mitch Pirtle

Book cover design by Kingwood Creations kingwoodcreations.com

Author photo courtesy of Lionel Madiou madious.com

I want to let you know that all my books and work as a holistic practitioner are a wholesome system, supporting you to live a more conscious, mindful, and happier life.

However, I made it so you can receive the benefit of living more joyously solely by working through this terrific journal book, while also experiencing the full satisfaction in continuing on to the next journal of this series—not to mention the rock solid tools you get by reading any of my other books or adding in my podcast *The Daily Freak*. Either way, I know you'll love my inspirational teachings.

Find out more at:
FreakyHealer.com
Amazon - Jacqueline Pirtle's Author Page
The Daily Freak Podcast

Before you dive in, I want to thank you for hopping on the positivity train with me! I truly hope you enjoy *The Silver Lining* as much as I loved writing it, and if you do, it would be wonderful if you could take a short minute to leave a review on Amazon and Goodreads.com as soon as you can.

Your kind feedback helps other readers find my books more easily, and to be happy faster. Consider it a joy-deed for the world.

Thank you!

ACKNOWLEDGMENTS

Let's be honest here… I have a dream team!

I could not have finished this book without the help of talented, creative, high-for-life, and phenomenal professionals.

From the bottom of my heart, I want to thank Zoe Pirtle for her editorial mastery; Mitch Pirtle for his all-round support; kingwoodcreations.com for their fun and polished book cover design; and madiouART.com for an amazing photo shoot.

I'd also like to extend a huge "Thank You!" to all fans of my work and books—I created this beautiful journal series for you.

Life is spectacular with you on my side!

Finding the silver lining is like living in a constant state of creme-de-la-creme.

DEDICATION

I dedicate this journal to all the downs in life!

May they become nothing else than another version of ups—magical, enriching, and growth initiating.

INTRODUCTION

Hello spectacular *silver liner*!

Let's clear this tiny little thought or big boulder that's on everyone's mind at some point:

Is the silver lining a state of denial?

No, it is not!

The silver lining is a conscious choice to experience life in the best way possible, suiting your whole being and nourishing your time here through whatever is going on for you right now—so you can show up as the best version of you that you can be while also having the most fun ever.

Never is it a superficial act to wash away burdens, hardships, and shocks in life. Instead, it is a very deeply and mindfully elected option to wizen up and rise to a growth in which you allow life to be, and take full responsibility for all that you are— then to freely and without judgment ask yourself:

- What does this happening mean FOR me?
- How do I feel in this experience?
- What energy am I in this situation?
- What frequency do I vibrate in while this is going on?

- What does the best version of me look like in this life event?
- How good - or how much better - could I feel, see, think, act, and live, right now?

The silver lining sits in between these questions and your answers—always right in front of you, and available at all times for you to make your brighter-side attitude your normal way of being and living.

You are so much more than just your physical you. You are also a soul, and ONE with consciousness—and as such you are invited to grow into *bigger* and *more* at all times in your humanness through the core of the energetic essence that makes everything and everyone.

Living in your own silver lining keeps you glued to your soul journey - one that you came here to live, in your most aligned and exuberant soul passionate ways - and this calibrates you higher and higher, pairing you with the grandest wisdom there is; meaning, you are experiencing life wholesomely as your complete being - body, mind, soul, and consciousness - where all pure positivity is held.

This *The Silver Lining* journal exists to support you in choosing brighter and more uplifting ways, the result being you will be happier, healthier, more positive, while also being more abundant energetically and from there new, fresh, and fitting solutions will present themselves easy peasy.

I say, let all your silver linings in so you can create a life where an ocean of opportunities will catch hold of you, and where swimming in such joy leaves you with a desire for more.

Journaling through this 30 day *The Silver Lining* gives your most uplifted version of you the spotlight, and brings a huge heightening into the equation so you can experience life like you never have before, craft a time beyond your dreams, and love what you live—so you can become a master in living consciously,

INTRODUCTION

mindfully, and feeling phenomenal while manifesting the best of the best. It's a change that is forever!

On a side note, there are a couple of bonus days at the end in case you ever find the need to do two entries in a day, or so you can keep writing while you wait for the next journal in this series to arrive. I also left you a few blank ***Silver Lining*** pages to journal about deepening your ways of being positively alive.

Enough chit-chat, I know you are ready—so grab your pen and have incredible fun catching more bliss than you have ever caught in your new and undoubted ways.

Happiest,
   Jacqueline

 ay 1

IMAGINE life being a voluminous space of emptiness, with two differently adventurous disks available to jump on at any time. Each disk has its own amazing experience of everything and everyone - all happenings, situations, people, and so on - and every new split second, you get to choose which disk you want to be on and live life through; plus, you can jump-change whenever you like.

Disk one mostly takes measures of what's happening on the physical life level, which can come with limited understanding—while disk two takes the energetic value that's based on the pure positive energy everything is at its core into account.

The latter disk is called the silver lining!

Here comes the fun! Close your eyes and imagine yourself in that spaciousness standing in front of those two incredible disks, cracking a smile and having an eagerness to live life to the fullest.

Which disk will you choose more often, and more mindfully?

___

The Silver Lining - And How to Find it

 ay 2

WHAT IS a silver lining for you? How do you feel about the brighter side? Is being optimistic something deep, or rather superficial for you?

Go on, this day is reserved for you to straighten out and beautify your relationship with all silver linings so that moving forward, you can take your victory dance of living more optimistically with pride and make this way part of your normal every day living.

The Silver Lining - And How to Find it

ay 3

Now that you have corrected any discrepancies and also rekindled your relationship with living on the brighter side - remember, at your energetic core you were, and are, always ONE with the silver lining - let's get into the business of your surroundings.

How are your surroundings structured—more on the positive, or more on the negative side? Without any judgement, or wanting to change your outer world, become aware of both disks being present and who's on what disk more often—also, who do you follow? Take note of that.

Then, with love and care latch onto the silver lining environments more often while leaving the tar-liners more and more out of your focus. Don't worry, you can still love them and stay close by—just not in a latching-on kind of way.

_____
_____
_____
_____
_____
_____
_____
_____
_____
_____
_____
_____
_____
_____

The Silver Lining - And How to Find it

 ay 4

WHEN SOMEONE or something new comes your way, what is your usual first response? Is it one filled with wonder and curiosity of what could be? Or is it the opposite—mistrust, hopelessness, or what-the-heck-ness? Start to really watch yourself and choose more optimism wherever you can.

The Silver Lining - And How to Find it

 Day 5

WHAT IN YOUR life is a drag? Why is it a drag? What is the silver lining in this drag of a happening? What is keeping you from living, and focusing on the brighter side?

___

The Silver Lining - And How to Find it

 Day 6

CHECK yourself and your thinking-ways often, to locate your old programmed ways that are unhelpful for you. Then, notice where you are putting these gunky habits.

What new and fresh living situations and experiences are you contaminating with these unhelpful beliefs?

What would the brighter silver lining viewpoint be?

___

The Silver Lining - And How to Find it

# Day 7

WHEN YOU HEAR the word *positivity* or the phrase "Be positive!" how are you feeling? Positive? A lot of times the automatic emotion that's present is actually of a negative nature because of old habits, rusty beliefs, and unhelpful ways.

Become consciously aware of your relationship with all *positivity* and align with its true essence, which is a beautifully cheerful energy.

The Silver Lining - And How to Find it

ay 8

CHOOSE A PHYSICAL SYMPTOM! Should not be hard, since they are a normal part of life and sometimes present in plentifulness.

Find the silver lining in the experience by creating an understanding of your physical evidence, and what it is communicating to you.

Make this a kind and friendly chat, since symptoms are the only way your physical body can talk it out with you!

If this is hard, keep practicing - and never give up - then pat yourself on the shoulder for a job well done.

___

The Silver Lining - And How to Find it

 ay 9

OKAY, so here is a silver lining spun into humor:

Imagine stepping into dog poop and thinking that this is a real hassle, but then turning it all around into, "My shoes can get some cleansing-love now, a shift into sparkliness and a shine that wasn't there before."

Yes, I understand that this one might take some real work, but I know that you can be an excellent *silver liner*, even during the poopy times. Bravo!

The Silver Lining - And How to Find it

ay 10

WHEN RECEIVING a bad meal - or cooking a not so enjoyable feast - how do you react? With frustration, most would assume. There are two silver linings in such a happening:

- You might get a free dessert out of the deal, or take-out-yumminess after all!
- A fire in you got lit—one that might have been dormant for a while. So yay for your annoyance!

Either way, go find your silver lining and make it count!

_____
_____
_____
_____
_____
_____
_____
_____
_____
_____
_____
_____
_____
_____
_____
_____
_____

The Silver Lining - And How to Find it

ay 11

You manifest from how you feel and think about things, while life brings you what is in accordance with your soul-needs for you to further your growth. That's THE silver lining!

What desire that's been on your mind is not coming through for you? Be specific with what it is, but don't go into the negativity of it not having happend yet. Is it a certain job that you really want, a house you have laid eyes on, or a relationship you are trying to make work?

So how DO you really feel about that missing link, and what are your true thoughts about it?

_____
_____
_____
_____
_____
_____
_____
_____
_____
_____
_____
_____
_____
_____
_____
_____

The Silver Lining - And How to Find it

 ay 12

A HEALTH CRISES is never ever *only* what it looks like on the physical life level—that's because you are a multi-level being, made of physical and energetic essences.

Any health happening is an invitation for a deep soul-self-care initiation, and a hint to align with the truest meaning of who you really are beyond your physical body.

Take that magnificent moment of light, reflect on this precious event, and find your silver lining: Your soul wisdom.

_____
_____
_____
_____
_____
_____
_____
_____
_____
_____
_____
_____
_____
_____
_____
_____
_____
_____
_____

The Silver Lining - And How to Find it

 ay 13

AUTUMN GIVES out free eye candy! Its beautiful colors and gorgeous tones during that time of year are the silver linings—because at the other end of the stick, is the mess of fall. What else in your nature-surroundings are such a clear shift to the bright side?

___

The Silver Lining - And How to Find it

 ay 14

LET'S stay a tiny bit longer with the fall season, and highlight the great change it represents and how refreshing and recharging letting go can be: A true silver lining!

What can you change? What changes are you wishing for? What can you let go of—what do you wish to go *poof*?

Simply just realizing where you're at on the scale of change, and what could be a goner for good, creates clarity and makes space for the new.

_____
_____
_____
_____
_____
_____
_____
_____
_____
_____
_____
_____
_____
_____
_____
_____
_____
_____
_____

The Silver Lining - And How to Find it

 Day 15

A LOT of beauty sits in sadness!

Embracing your wonderful sad emotions means that you are lining up with the bright parts of these moments, and allows the cleansing of your huge heart to take place, while also creating limitless strength and amazing clarity of who you really are.

How will you celebrate your sadness more often?

___

The Silver Lining - And How to Find it

 ay 16

ANGER BRINGS up powerful silver linings, because this strong feeling is a warrior type essence—and everyone is capable of experiencing it.

I say, why not let your warrior out a bit more often, instead of bottling it up or putting a "being bad" stamp on it?

Of course it's understood that nobody should get hurt by doing so—choose a time when you are alone and then get to it.

The Silver Lining - And How to Find it

 ay 17

JEALOUSY IS your truth barometer of what you really desire for yourself. Why? It's not a shareable energy - nobody can share their jealousy with you, and you can't share yours either - whereas anger, sadness, or happiness are all shared and spread all the time; hence, when you are happy you light up the room, et cetera.

That makes jealousy purely yours!

What are you jealous about? Who are you jealous of? Really dig deep here, and let it flow 100%.

Voila, you have your wish marching orders! How will you start down this silver lined path?

_____
_____
_____
_____
_____
_____
_____
_____
_____
_____
_____
_____
_____
_____
_____
_____
_____

The Silver Lining - And How to Find it

 ay 18

Even happiness has a deeper silver lining, because why in the world would you stop at feeling amazing when the next level is to consciously create even more joy, and feel even higher, in the bliss department?

The silver lining? There is never a ceiling to how amazing you can BE and live!

_____
_____
_____
_____
_____
_____
_____
_____
_____
_____
_____
_____
_____
_____
_____
_____
_____
_____
_____
_____

The Silver Lining - And How to Find it

ay 19

CRY A LITTLE MORE!

Shedding tears is often looked at as weak, not in control, emotionally disturbed, erratic, or not capable. That's not true and I hope deep down we all know that, even if these old beliefs and habits linger around the world.

The silver lining of weeping is that it's an act of cleansing—energetically, physically, emotionally, and as a whole.

What is your relationship with sobbing—as the cryer, or even when others shed their tears?

_____
_____
_____
_____
_____
_____
_____
_____
_____
_____
_____
_____
_____
_____
_____
_____
_____

The Silver Lining - And How to Find it

 ay 20

WHAT LITTLE THINGS in your life do you enjoy? Make a long list!

What are the silver linings - besides making you happy - of these petite happenings or objects? How do you feel in these tiny bliss-moments? What are your thoughts when you are being so jolly?

The Silver Lining - And How to Find it

 ay 21

WHAT HUMONGOUS THINGS do you enjoy in your life? Make your big list!

What is the silver lining of these huge attributes, and what emotions do they create for you?

Could you go for even bigger things in life?

___

The Silver Lining - And How to Find it

ay 22

THERE ARE days when you want to go slow because it feels good to be the essence of a snail, and there are moments when being a speedster is the perfect way to live.

Your silver lining here is to match your speed to your deserved ways of feeling good.

Important! That is the case for everyone—so next time, when someone cuts in front of you, know that their silver lining is *speed* while your silver lining is to stick to the pace that's best for you. Take the invitation to reevaluate if you are indeed at your fitting speed. For instance, if you are annoyed, speed up too!

The Silver Lining - And How to Find it

 ay 23

KNOWING when to be fully involved and even being the life of the party, or when to pull back so you can reconnect with yourself and evaluate your alignment with your truth, is the silver lining in every single adventurous split second of being alive.

What type of *silver liner* are you right now - the partier or the hermiter - and does it fit? How will you make it more YOU, more often?

___

The Silver Lining - And How to Find it

 ay 24

WHEN THERE IS a detour or delay, know that the bump in your plan-road is keeping or directing you to where you need to be. Maybe just maybe there is traffic ahead, an accident to be avoided, or a new place to be discovered.

How can you react more on the silver lining side next time this happens?

The Silver Lining - And How to Find it

Day 25

EVERY BREATH - GOING IN, and going out - has silver lining wisdom included!

Try it! Breathe in and ask, "What's the silver lining in *this* or *that*?" then breathe out, and notice the answers flowing in for you.

This is a practice of deep gratitude and love!

The Silver Lining - And How to Find it

ay 26

EXHAUSTION! We all know how it feels.

The silver lining in being tired to the core is that your wholesome you - both the physical and energetic - is guiding you to rest, relax, and be in your peacefulness.

How can you give in to this amazing brilliance more often?

The Silver Lining - And How to Find it

 ay 27

STOMACH FLU—WE love you, we love you not!

Could you possibly see the silver lining in a good ol' intestinal disturbance? I sure hope so, because it's not just a cleansing of your physical body, but also energetically, to reboot your system and start fresh. Of course this counts for food poisoning as well —but please, if you need medical assistance, use common sense and go see a doctor!

The Silver Lining - And How to Find it

ay 28

HAVING a mop of hair that turns you into a shaggy dog has a beautiful silver lining because you get to go beautify yourself, hang out with someone who loves their craft, and come out of it better than before—or at least that's the hope.

Yet, many times this outing starts with, "Oh my, I have to go to the haircutter *again!*"

Make this frequent silver lining count, since it happens almost every month—or even more!

The Silver Lining - And How to Find it

 ay 29

ARE you denying the beauty of silver linings? Newsflash, everyone does at some point leaving the remaining question:

Is this a once in a while behavior, or your normal way of being and living?

Oh, and one more thought to ponder—why would it even be your regular mode of operations to refuse the bright side?

The Silver Lining - And How to Find it

 ay 30

YOUR SILVER LINING is never about anything else but YOU, and it does not include others or anything outside of yourself. Ever!

How will you stay within your own personal silver zone at all times?

_____
_____
_____
_____
_____
_____
_____
_____
_____
_____
_____
_____
_____
_____
_____
_____
_____
_____
_____
_____

The Silver Lining - And How to Find it

* * *

Ready to continue on your self-growth path? Get the next journal in this series: ***Money - The Gift That Gives***

BONUS

Because hey, no one ever wants the goodness to end.

The silver lining is no joke!
Then again, why not bring on the silly!

 ay 31

How cool is it, that everything in life has a silver lining at all times?!?

Close your eyes and take a deep breath, then ask yourself and the co-creational universe, "What is my main silver lining for my new day?"

Do this every morning for a week, and see what happens!

The Silver Lining - And How to Find it

ay 32

TAKE your golden time to practice becoming a professional *silver liner*! But beware, nobody said "wait for diamonds before choosing the sparkly side."

Your NOW is all you have available! So *silver-up*, capable one!

The Silver Lining - And How to Find it

 ay 33

How many times are you going to choose to BE and live on the bright side today? Once, ten times, or one hundred precent?

Will you give in to your talents of looking for the silver lining and follow this positivity trend that's yours to live?

Please say "Yes!"

The Silver Lining - And How to Find it

 ay 34

THE PRACTICE of being a *silver liner* means that you become ONE with everything, and create a pure space where your physical essence can meet your energetical essence, and as such be one with consciousness. It's a brightness of magnitude!

Try it! Close your eyes and lay your body flat—breathe yourself into your bright side. Once there, sense how you are ONE with everything. Embrace that deep relaxation and realize that, right then and there, you are filled to the brim with the silver linings of all there is: Energy!

Are you there yet?

The Silver Lining - And How to Find it

 ay 35

SILVER LINERS ARE SOMETIMES ALSO nay-sayers, negative-ers, and down-ers—and that's normal, since we're all a bunch of mixed personalities.

Brush off all negative ways - yours and those of other people - and let them go with your bestest *okay-ness* and normalness. Then, turn your focus towards your brighter side where you love yourself enough to create more silver linings to enjoy.

The Silver Lining - And How to Find it

AND NOW IT'S YOUR TURN!

The following are your silver pages to become happier and jollier as we speak, or rather, as you write!

 ay 36

MY FAVORITE SILVER LININGS ARE…

The Silver Lining - And How to Find it

# Day 37

THE FUNNY SILVER LININGS CREATE...

The Silver Lining - And How to Find it

ay 38

WHEN FINDING my own silver linings I feel…

The Silver Lining - And How to Find it

Day 39

BEING A *SILVER LINER* STARTS WITH…

The Silver Lining - And How to Find it

 ay 40

Silver linings are capable of healing…

___

The Silver Lining - And How to Find it

* * *

Don't forget to leave a review on Amazon.com and Goodreads.com as soon as you can, as your kind feedback helps other readers find my books easier. Thank you!

ALSO BY JACQUELINE PIRTLE

365 Days of Happiness

Because happiness is a piece of cake!

This passage book invites you to create a daily habit to live your every day joy, and is the parent companion to *365 Days of Happiness*, the journal workbook.

* * *

365 Days of Happiness - Special Edition

Because happiness is a piece of cake

This beautiful Special Edition of the bestseller *365 Days of Happiness: Because happiness is a piece of cake* has room for your notes after every daily passage.

* * *

365 Days of Happiness - Journal Workbook

Because happiness is a piece of cake

This enlightening journal workbook is your daily tool to create a habit of living your every day bliss, and is the companion to *365 Days of Happiness: Because happiness is a piece of cake*.

* * *

Life IS Beautiful - Here's to New Beginnings

If you like digging deeper into the meaning of life and are inspired by spirituality, then you'll love Jacqueline's effective teachings.

* * *

Parenting Through the Eyes of Lollipops

A Guide to Conscious Parenting

If you like harmony at home and laughter in the house, then you'll love Jacqueline's inspirational methods.

* * *

What it Means to BE a Woman

And Yes! Women do Poop!

If you like to live free, empowered, and want to decide for yourself, then you'll love Jacqueline's liberating ways.

* * *

Life-changing Journals

What. If. - Turning your IFs into it IS!

Open - Where it all starts!

To BE and Live - The reason you are here!

High for Life - The best case scenario!

Bragging - Because you're worth it!

Of Course - Because why wait...

Align, Expand, and Calibrate - Your Stairway to Joy

Magick and Broomsticks - The Portal to Your Wild Side

Money - The Gift That Gives

Every journal comes in two lengths:

A 30 day journal - A 90 day journal, The Extended Edition

If you like being in charge of your own life, turning your dreams into reality, enjoy journaling, and want to squeeze the most out of your time, then you'll love Jacqueline's uplifting teachings.

ABOUT THE AUTHOR

Bestselling author, podcaster, and holistic practitioner, Jacqueline Pirtle, has twenty-four years of experience helping thousands of clients discover their own happiness. Jacqueline is the owner of *FreakyHealer* and has shared her solid teachings through her podcast *The Daily Freak*, sessions, workshops, presentations, and books with clients all over the world. She holds international degrees in holistic health and natural living. Her effective healing work has been featured in print and online magazines, podcasts, radio shows, on TV, and in the documentary *The Overly Emotional Child by Learning Success*, available on Amazon Prime.

For any questions you might have, to sign up for Jacqueline's newsletter, and for more information on whatever else she is up to, visit www.freakyhealer.com and her social media accounts @freakyhealer.

www.ingramcontent.com/pod-product-compliance
Lightning Source LLC
Chambersburg PA
CBHW071423070526
44578CB00003B/674